PLATFORM PAPERS

QUARTERLY ESSAYS ON THE PERFORMING ARTS FROM CURRENCY HOUSE

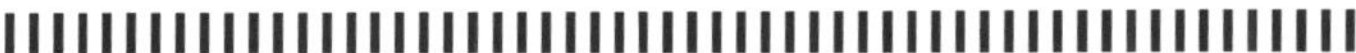

No. 43
May 2015

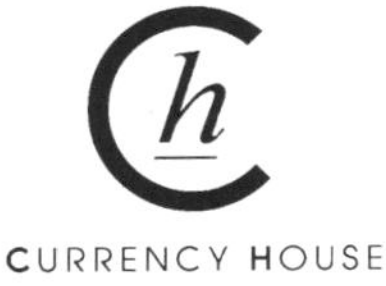

Platform Papers Partners

We acknowledge with gratitude our Partners in continuing support of Platform Papers and its mission to widen understanding of performing arts practice and encourage change when it is needed:

Gillian Appleton
Anita Luca Belgiorno Nettis Foundation
Jane Bridge
Katharine Brisbane, AM
Elizabeth Butcher, AM
Penny Chapman
Robert Connolly
Peter Cooke, OAM
Rowena Cowley and Dr Richard Letts, AM
Michael J. Crouch, AO
Ian Enright
Larry Galbraith
Tony Grierson
Gail Hambly
Wayne Harrison, AM
Campbell Hudson
Professors Bruce King and Denise Bradley, AC
Peter Lee
Roderick H. McGeoch, AO
David Marr
Harold Mitchell, AC, AO
Joanna Murray-Smith
Helen O'Neil
Martin Portus
Professor William Purcell
Geoffrey Rush, AC
Dr Merilyn Sleigh
Positive Solutions
Seaborn Broughton Walford Foundation
Augusta Supple
Andrew Upton
Rachel Ward, AM and Bryan Brown, AM
Kim Williams, AM
Professor Di Yerbury, AM

To them and to all subscribers and Friends of Currency House we extend our grateful thanks.

Platform Papers Readers' Forum

Readers' responses to our essays will from now on be posted on our website.

Currency House invites readers to send us considered responses to this or previous Platform Papers in length between 250 and 2000 words. Submissions may be emailed to info@currencyhouse.org.au with a brief biographical note. The Editor welcomes opinion and criticism in the interest of healthy debate but reserves the right to monitor where necessary.

Platform Papers, quarterly essays on the performing arts, are published every February, May, August and November and are available through bookshops, by subscription and on line in paper or electronic version. For details see our website at www.currencyhouse.org.au.

THE ARTS AND THE COMMON GOOD

KATHARINE BRISBANE

ACKNOWLEDGEMENTS

This book is dedicated to all the Platform Papers authors who have worked with John Golder and myself over the past ten years and more, to build this series; and to John, who conceived the series and led it until 2012. Their knowledge and hard-won experience have illuminated many dark corners of our artists' life and practice and shown us all a way forward; and for that I am truly grateful.

In the writing of no.43, I have had the assistance of a handful of wise counsellors. Firstly my daughter Harriet Parsons, who has been my best editor and literary adviser since Philip left us; and my old friends Julian Meyrick, an artist with a metaphor, and quick to see through a weak argument or unsubstantiated claim; and John Senczuk, who like me has lived the history I have plumbed. Both these men are already Platform Papers authors and enjoyed the opportunity of being as frank with my text as I was with theirs. Also Cathy Hunt, soon to be, like Julian, a Platform Papers author for a second time, who was a challenging critic and guided me through a minefield of opinion on government policy and financial practice. I also express my gratitude to Michael Campbell, now chair of our editorial committee, for his determination that I should write this paper, and for his last-minute proof-reading. And to the editorial committee itself:

Robin Derricourt, Julian Meyrick, Martin Portus, Nick Shimmin and Greig Tillotson, for their continuing dedication and good conversation.

Lastly, my special thanks go to my right hand at Currency House, Priscilla Yates, whose management skills, timely research and vigilance have enabled me to complete this paper. For that and all the other things she does for Currency House, she has my lasting gratitude.

About the Author

Katharine Brisbane is a writer and publisher who co-founded Currency Press, Australia's performing arts publisher, with her late husband, Dr Philip Parsons, in 1971. She was a theatre critic for 21 years, including a period as national critic of the *Australian* (1967–1974), a time of radical change that saw the rise of contemporary drama, film and music in Australia. She has published widely on the history and nature of Australian theatre. She remained publisher of Currency Press until her retirement in 2001 and at that time established Currency House, Inc., a not-for-profit association with the brief to assert the value of the performing arts in public life and raise the level of debate.

She was a founder in 1972 of the Australian National Playwrights' Conference and was Chair from 1985–1990. In 1991 to celebrate Currency Press's first twenty years she edited *Entertaining Australia,* a social history of the performing arts. In 1993 Katharine and Philip were both awarded the AM for their work as publishers of Australian drama. Dr Parsons died the same month and Katharine completed the production of his encyclopaedia, *Companion to Theatre in Australia*, published in 1995. She holds honorary doctorates from the University of NSW and the University of WA, and many awards for her writing and publishing, including the Dorothy Crawford

Award by the Australian Writers' Guild for outstanding service to the Australian playwright, and lifetime achievement awards from Melbourne's Green Room, the Sydney Critics Circle, and in 2009 a Special Award from the NSW Premier in the Literary Awards list for services to Australian literature and theatre.

From 1994 she was editor for the South Pacific for the *World Encyclopaedia of Contemporary Theatre* (Routledge), for which she also wrote the Australian entry. Volume 5: *Asia and the Pacific* was published in 1998. She has written widely in books and journals and a collection of her writings, *Not Wrong, Just Different: Observations on the rise of the contemporary theatre,* was published in 2005.

Katharine Brisbane has two children: Nicholas, a filmmaker, and Harriet, an artist; and two granddaughters.

Introduction

Not long ago, while my younger granddaughter was staying with me, her partner brought her a bunch of multi-coloured cabbage roses. At first I thought they were artificial but a touch showed me they were real cream roses that had been dyed.

I was affronted. And then I was surprised at the strength of my response. Is this art? I asked myself. What was the meaning of this act? To my mind it was vandalism: the florist had changed a perfect rose into a stage impersonation. But then there was another question. Was the rose itself not already a work of art or even artifice? A work created by years of careful breeding by the gardener?

On reflection it is not the despoiled roses that offended me but the values they represented. That the roses were not valued sufficiently in their own right but needed human intervention to make them special, more 'valuable' in cultural and pecuniary terms. What was now their value?

Art makes us think about what we value. This is essential to a healthy society. The difference between a commodity and a work of art, between a bunch of beautifully contrived multi-coloured roses and Jeff Koons' *Puppy* on the Sydney Harbour foreshore, is whether it makes us reflect upon our culture, individually and through this gift of exchange. But the roses were given and received uncritically, were not communally shared, and so the lesson was lost. They had not succeeded in contributing to a larger aesthetic, as a purposeful work made up of artificial or sculptured flowers might have been. They lacked 'art'. Meanwhile the rosebush simply regenerates, brings to life other roses, perhaps more beautiful than the last.

The value of great art accrues through little acts of reflection. Over time we learn to articulate this value, to analyse its aesthetics, to define what we call 'community standards'. Some time, perhaps in the 1980s, 'grow' became a transitive verb that could be applied to commerce. If I said I was 'growing flowers' it used to mean I had planted them. Now we talk about 'growing' a business, as if an owner can simply decide to make a profit. We can cultivate our art and our culture but we cannot 'grow' its value or its popularity. No amount of calculation or modelling can guarantee success and it is arrogant of us to claim it. Success, if it comes, comes as a surprise and a gift. Using 'grow' as transitive in a commercial context turns cultivation into a kind of manufacturing.

The relationship between art and money has been a contested one since commerce was invented. And as demeaning as despoiling a rose—or a work of art—for the purpose of profit. We do it all the time, of course. The artist's need to live decently is as great as the entrepreneur's. But when it comes to the common good, the struggle is an unequal one: the more generous the public becomes towards the artist, the more extravagant or subversive the art is likely to be.

The problem is that 'the arts', as we Westerners express it, is itself an artificial construct, represented by both art and commerce. When I first visited Bali in 1973 our interpreter was curious about the opening of the Sydney Opera House. What was this building? What was its purpose? Balinese had no need for such a building, he said; they had no word for 'the arts', only for their practices; and no word for the stage or a special purpose building. Their practice was everywhere. In Bali at that time there appeared to be no practical distinction made between art and commerce, only around the quality of the work. The great artists had their lavish studios; the small artisans their market stalls. But the cultural value of their intent was taken for granted, whatever the end purpose of the product. Robyn Archer has famously written: 'What artists produce, the end result of what they do, is the detritus of the creative process.'[1] The tourist industry being what it is, the Balinese must have a whole vocabulary for these things by now.

So how do we compare Australia's understanding and appreciation of art with that of Bali, for example? How do we distinguish between art and commodity? What do we mean by investment? My daughter Harriet and I have been debating these questions for twenty years. She is an artist who, having worked as a bookkeeper over the years, came to notice how accounting has appropriated the language of emotions: 'redemption', 'reconciliation', 'interest'. She developed her thoughts into an argument on the emotional language of accounting, which traces the distinctions between the commercial transaction and the emotions of ownership that accompany long-term investment. In doing so she comments on Adam Smith's *Theory of Moral Sentiments* (his *first* book) to show how culture supplies the values exchanged in the financial economy:

> *Instead of profit, loss, assets and liabilities, Smith's* Moral Sentiments *weighs its values in the balance of four moral attitudes: self-interest, competition, reputation and self-respect. Each of these attitudes reflects a point of view: how we see ourselves, how others appear to us, how we appear to others and how we imagine we appear in their eyes. [...]'Investment' means literally 'to put on as a garment', to take on an identity. When I 'invest' in a book of poems by Coleridge, I take on an identity that changes the way I see myself, how others appear to me, how I appear to them and how I imagine I appear in their eyes.*[2]

The value of this investment depends on the culture, she continues:

> *For an Australian, reading the poetry of Coleridge is not [necessarily] an investment in English culture but a re-investment in the ties of colonialism. Cultivating an appreciation for Coleridge's poetry is not enough to decide whether this investment in our heritage constitutes a growth or loss of Australian identity. Perspective requires the context of history.*

Culture is inherited, and in Australia this investment in our own culture has been inhibited by factors that can be traced back to colonial times: a lack of confidence to do with being a largely immigrant nation, with low education prospects, eager for others to teach us how to 'appreciate' (another accounting term) our culture. Our Indigenous population doesn't have such problems with their own culture, of course, only in understanding the one we have imposed. Recently I read again Donald Horne's *The Lucky Country*. It is fifty years since it was published and it no longer has the power to shock but it remains an extraordinarily percipient character study of Australian life and its aspirations. About our culture (still at this time overwhelmingly Anglo-Celtic) he writes of the pervasive influence of our colonial past and role as a member of the British Commonwealth:

> *Australians learn their culture. They learn it as if it described their own life and attitudes, when in part it does not, and this process seems to make the relevant in the culture they learn also unreal. This sense of unreality can affect even those who have learned their culture very thoroughly: they cannot detect the difference between their own society and the societies of the culture they have learned. [...] He is déclassé, unable to talk to other Australians of the culture he has learned because he lacks a real feel for both it and his own society.*[3]

Horne's book was written before the transformational changes of the 1960s took hold, and long before the children of the post-war—and post many wars—immigrants have come to take such a prominent place in Australian society. But what he says is still true. We older settlers have had to 'learn' our history because the last 227 years have been so contested. We were firstly a British penal colony, then an agricultural one. Then quasi self-governing, then assimilationist, then multi-cultural; then relativist. Once begging for immigrants, now forcing them away. Will we ever understand our 'true' history or our 'own' people? We intruders have even succeeded in destroying a good part of the story of our original inhabitants.

Too few of us give our history the attention it deserves because there is so much still to be understood and opinion keeps changing. Despite our being inveterate travellers, with an intense if superficial fascination with the history and culture of other countries, those immigrant generations active in public life today have succeeded in great part not because they have added colour to our parochial lives but because their surname is the only apparently foreign thing about them.

Horne was also writing before federal government began to take a policy interest in the arts. From that time what had been a generally accepted, if undefined, view—that some things were part of popular culture and others were, or aspired to be, art—became by degrees a field for research, criticism and regulation. It came to be called relativism.

Back in 1967 I became the infant *Australian's* national theatre critic, and recorded the controversies that surrounded the unfamiliar concept of a national performing arts industry.[4] For the last ten years, as publisher of these Platform Papers, I have had my attention drawn again and again to the consequences of those early ambitions. Each paper has taught me much and consecutively they add to a subtext of views that point ominously to a single conclusion.

It was Wesley Enoch in his Platform Paper (no.40) that prompted me to explore the emerging pattern and to ask: have we followed the right path?

As times change and the role of our larger companies shifts, should we not re-investigate why they exist and what role they should play in our country? [...] Surely in fifty years from now when some of our companies will be celebrating their centenary, we will not be still expecting them to stay the same.[5]

Every business needs a review from time to time. In 2017 it will be 50 years since the first steps were taken to form what became the Australia Council. It's time we looked at our early aspirations and the structure we built to support them.

The original vision in itself was flawed. I know because I was there.

1 The beginnings

It all began with the Sydney Opera House, looking back. The pursuit of excellence. My story begins in 1968 but by that time its foundations had been laid and a change of state government had brought down its architect in a storm of anger and ridicule. Here we were with a world-famous building we didn't know how to finish, an opera company without an orchestra, under the shabby umbrella of the Australian Elizabethan Theatre Trust; and an infant Australian Ballet company just finding its feet under the direction of Peggy Van Praagh and Robert Helpmann. Neither had the resources to occupy the grand premises being prepared for them; and they quickly lost ownership of their opera theatre to the ABC Concert Department on the evidence of the latter's known quality and tight subscription system.[6] (It is now the Concert Hall.) Meanwhile in this city classic theatre was represented by various semi-professional groups, until, in 1964, a hundred-seat Old Tote Theatre was converted out of an old racecourse totalisator as a facility for the new National Institute of Dramatic Art. These were the elements waiting to shine in what has come to be known as the Eighth Wonder of the World. It was this curious collection of talents that set alight the dream of greatness and took the first shaky steps towards its realisation.

Performing arts, back in 1968, when the first incarnation of the Australia Council was initiated, consisted of the ABC concert seasons, with the local ABC orchestras and the best available solo artists from abroad; J.C. Williamson's (JCW), the vast commercial monopoly that presented us with the best musicals and comedies from Broadway and the West End; and the failing Australian Elizabethan Theatre Trust, Australia's first formal attempt at public subsidy for the arts. The Trust, as it was known, was grossly under-resourced and by this time had formed a partnership with JCW, who managed the Trust's Australian Ballet and Elizabethan Opera. The struggling Ballet was itself a makeover of the Borovansky Ballet following the death of Boro in 1959.[7] Beyond these was a lively amateur or semi-professional community, led by actors from British and American touring companies who had found a home here, and the European immigrant community who had fled to Australia firstly in the pre-war period and then under the post-war immigration plan. Notable among these was Richard Goldner, a salesman and violist who formed a small string orchestra in 1939 that became Musica Viva; Sidney Myer, a salesman who generated a fortune that still resonates on behalf of the arts today; and Gertrud Bodenweiser, a modern dance exponent from the Max Reinhardt circle in Vienna, whose legacy has informed the whole trajectory of modern dance in Australia.

All these immigrant generations contributed enormously to this country. Their artisan skills and business acumen built careers to support them, and liquidity with which to express their artistic knowledge and become generous and informed patrons. Australia still benefits from these families and the children who inherited their understanding of the contribution music, literature, dance and drama make to a civilised society.

The arts they cultivated, however, were largely European, motivated by a need in some way to share with their new community those things they had valued and lost. The growth of an indigenous style of performing arts had a different kind of struggle, one to recognise and celebrate who we thought we were, what was distinctive about the culture we had nurtured so far from our countries of origin. These influences did not have the ancient, aristocratic roots of the imported culture; instead they shared those of a multifarious colonial society: egalitarian, self-determined, populist. From the 1850s strolling players had taken ship for Australia to relieve the population of the gold that filled the cities' vaults. They brought their own ballads and melodramas and quickly improvised on local themes and practices. Vaudeville became a home for lampooning the pretentious and authoritarian; a voice of comic criticism that survives today in different motley.

From the 1920s the infant film industry began to document the landscape and the life of Australians in its silent and then sound movies, and most notably its newsreels; and as education expanded came the beginnings of a body of literature, composition and isolated attempts by middle-class aspirants to create an Australian drama. Famously the playwright Louis Esson, on seeking advice in Ireland from the Abbey Theatre's pioneers of a national theatre, was advised to go home and write plays about 'all those men going mad in lonely huts'.[8] But his Pioneer Players were a tame lot, unable to face the consequences of letting the genie out of the bottle. Katharine Susannah Prichard's play *Brumby Innes*, exposing the brutal miscegenation of at least one pioneering outback cattleman, won a literary prize in 1927 but no performance. Betty Roland fared better from the Melbourne Repertory Society with her *The Touch of Silk* (1928) which dealt with post-traumatic stress disorder, or shell-shock, as it was then called, and rural prejudice, sexual hunger and isolation; but in less blunt terms than Prichard.

There were no openings for writers in the theatre outside the amateur movements. The 'serious' theatre—the kind which the Australia Council spearheaded with the establishment of the state companies some forty years later—was in the hands of small part-amateur enterprises that filled the gap in our education with plays by Shaw, Moliere, Ibsen, Chekhov, Odets; and experimented in European, Japanese and Chinese theatre. But they rarely produced contemporary Australian writers. Moreover J.C. Williamson's, as Julian Meyrick pointed out in his Platform Paper (no.39), invested in their plays and musicals ready-to-wear, and, if truth be told, never knew how to develop a production from the page. The director (or producer as he/she was then called) was an invention of the twentieth century and a director-driven production was a rare exception.

There was one new avenue of employment through this time: radio. Radio began in the 1930s and drama, comedy and popular music were given a boost on outbreak of war when the Government froze the Australian earnings of international companies. So Lux Radio and Colgate Palmolive began presenting home-grown dramas and built for writers and actors a profitable industry of radio plays and serials that lasted until the arrival of television in 1956. An important by-product of this was the opportunity it offered classic vaudevillians, notably the lovable George Wallace, Roy Rene (Mo), with his disreputable character Mo McCackey and his motley crew, and other comedians and character actors, to disseminate a distinctive style of rough, indigenous radio comedy based on Steele Rudd's Dad and Dave characters, and the stories of Henry Lawson and C.J. Dennis. Sadly, this low comedy style did not extend to the middle-class amateur theatre. I think it was Colin Ballantyne, Adelaide's leader of theatre culture in the post-war period, who commented: 'There was an elocution teacher in every suburb.'

Self-consciousness about the Australian accent was strong and remained so until the late 1960s when the New Wave arrived and actors who could 'do' a good accent and show some muscle found themselves in demand. Kath Leahy, in her compelling history of class and accent in our theatre, says it is still hard to find a natural accent on stage or screen, because of the class pressures behind its expression.[9]

By the 1950s the repertory companies, or little theatres, as they were called—groups with their own theatres, professional management and unpaid actors—were making moves to become professional. Their motives were still largely social, and their repertoire was comedy and farce, with an occasional contemporary European play in translation. Australian writing was given a go sporadically. Only the socialist New Theatre movement embraced it emphatically.

So when in 1949 the Australian Government began to take an interest in the arts, after the first wave of the arts for peace movement had reached Australia and the British Council's emissary, Tyrone Guthrie, had taken a fortnight's jaunt through our capitals, no one was surprised that he recommended that our best and brightest be sent to the UK to be properly trained in body and voice. So they did and they were. The 50s and 60s were blessed by the chaotic and inept era of the Australian Elizabethan Theatre Trust, which supported this emigration; and by default cultivated a substantial generation of performers of international repute.[10]

But in all these endeavours the voice of the playwright, the composer, the choreographer, could be heard only occasionally. Ray Lawler, John Antill, Robert Helpmann are just three who succeeded but continued to hold an ambivalent attitude towards their country and their profession for the rest of their lives.

2. The 1960s revolution

The call of Australia was always there, of course, unconsciously expressive and unself-conscious. While Antill at the ABC was fighting to get airtime for our struggling composers, the rock industry had been growing and, as the baby boomer generation reached their majority in the mid-1960s along with the Beatles, Bob Dylan and the Vietnam War, the heady mix incited a scatter-gun protest movement, expressed in a conflation of rock and blues ballads; in plays, painting and, notably, the revival of a film industry.

The fact that almost all of this work was iconoclastic was inevitable, given our history. The turmoil of the late 1960s was the catalyst for a shake-up in almost every aspect of civic and private life and energised a youthful spirit of confidence and revolt. It was the atmosphere of dissention and demand that activated the government into funding the first stage of the Australia Council in 1968; what followed, looking back, was equally inevitable.

By this time J.C. Williamson's—its managers, the enterprising Tait brothers long gone—was falling prey to the brash new rock musicals and other entrepreneurs like Kenn Brodziak and the dynamic Harry M. Miller. It died unmourned in 1976. Its protégé, the AETT, had been founded in 1954, in a very different social climate, with public and private funds raised on a 3:1 basis, but by this time had cut back their expensive touring and did little beyond keep a token presence outside Sydney and Melbourne. The Trust had been, and still was, in active partnership with the Union Theatre Repertory Company (now the Melbourne Theatre Company), the Old Tote Theatre Company in Sydney and the South Australian Theatre Company; it housed the Marionette Theatre of Australia and the Theatre of the Deaf and had supported the founding of the National Institute of Dramatic Art in 1959–60. It also provided what was then a single channel for tax deductible donations to the arts.[11] Though now failing, the Trust had for nearly twenty years wielded considerable political power —and latterly an equal amount of ignominy, as the rising tide of dissent against their reactionary opinions grew in the latter years of the 1960s. A new umbrella for these organisations had to be devised.

Ballet afficionado and chairman of the Reserve Bank Dr Nugget Coombs and his colleagues grasped the opportunity of a divided government (following the retirement in 1966 of Sir Robert Menzies) to push for change. His most urgent call was to save the flagging fortunes of the AETT-supported companies. And he was successful in winning seeding funding. With no time to waste he drew up a series of boards, by genre, and set about nominating the guidelines. Pop music, already growing into an industry, was hastily excluded, as was 'commercial' theatre.

That was the moment when we might have reviewed the requirements of an infant arts sector presented with a brief like Rumplestiltskin's, to spin straw into gold.

But Australia was still in the hands of the old school, the 'self-appointed entrepreneurs' as Tim Rowse called them in his genial paperback, *Arguing the Arts*:

> *The Trust's early policy of touring gives a clue to one of the beliefs that animated this generation of entrepreneurs. They thought that in Australia, and especially outside the two largest cities, people were starved of culture. Australian society 'was characterised by a good-natured and resourceful philistinism which could be challenged by presentation of what the Trust believed was the best of European culture.*[12]

This was the origin of the Australia Council's avowed aim: 'the pursuit of excellence'. But the real issue was not whether those resourceful philistines needed this cultural conversion but from whence this steady stream of excellence would come.

The career path of performer, traditionally, was to learn by performing—performing for anyone who would employ them, in circus, dance companies, melodrama houses or concert hall. The opportunity to show and advance your skills was the purpose. Why suddenly was it assumed that 'high art' would not pay its way, and that commercial management did not deserve our respect and subsidy? Who decided this? The grave councillors. Pop music had the better part by being excluded, having built up their own cottage industry, won and lost fortunes and made the winning worth the while. The screen industry, after a brief burst of radicalism, was caught between the two.

Coombs had said at the time that he wanted to avoid a monolith, that there should be 'many doors' to success for his artists. And for a while there were. The original Council was not a single building but scattered; it appointed artists as field officers employed to be mentors and scouts, to gather information and report back. They advised on opportunities and tutored applicants on their submissions. Artists' hopes were high. Meanwhile the Council staff were enduring harsh and persistent criticism from the mystified public; and in the end hunkered down in Sydney. In the tussle for position and funds familiar faces reappeared at the helm in a new guise. A divide grew between the needy and those charged with answering that need: The rules and deadlines became immutable—though till the end of the 1980s the more understanding Council staff still found a way around them. Looking back, it was probably the best that could be done.

The frenzied pace of change was mirrored in the creative activity. The protest marches for which the late 1960s became notorious were against our involvement in the Vietnam War but also against censorship of both international (mainly French) films and the rough home-grown features of the reborn industry. A raw vernacular, sometimes transcending in its capacity for metaphor, became grist for both film and the experimental plays at La Mama, Jane Street, Tribe, PACT and many other makeshift venues. In the late 60s a series of challenges to the censorship laws were made, by both local plays and commercial productions of *Hair* and Mart Crowley's censor-challenging gay comedy *The Boys in the Band.*

Actors were arrested, following complaints of obscenity, with little result, and a few venues were closed on grounds of public safety. It was all part of the clearing out of worn-out public attitudes and unquestioned regulation—the stasis of old men too long in office.

By this time both the Australian Performing Group in Melbourne and Nimrod Street Theatre in Sydney, along with similar, less well documented, movements in the other capitals, had begun to be recognised as symptoms of a new young Australia demanding to be heard. The rising excitement had convinced the dying federal government of a cultural renaissance and given strength to the belief of the naïve young ideologues that, with seeding funding, a sunrise of the arts would dawn if they showed the way.

In 1972 the Australian Labor Party (ALP) won the federal election for the first time in 23 years. Funding to the infant Council was tripled and the New Wave began to roll.

3. Continued guardianship

In the years between then and now, the Australia Council has gone through many revolutions, in the expectation that it could make things better for our artists. And sometimes for a while they have. But gratitude has continued to elude the good intentions. Like most of the institutions they encouraged, the original visionaries are gone and their names barely remembered.

Gone also is the impetus for the structure on which the Council was based. When the state theatre companies were established between 1969 and 1973, most of the artistic directors were British-trained.[13] And the structure of their work and their buildings followed the English repertory pattern that had gone before. The notable exception was Hayes Gordon, the American musical star who had founded the Ensemble Theatre in Sydney in 1959 and introduced to Australia in-the-round playing and the gritty realism of the Strasberg School.[14] (Gordon refused to convert to the non-profit structure and the Ensemble has continued as a successful, privately supported business to this day.)

Soon the 'many doors' were closing. The Council's slogan, 'the pursuit of excellence', was an aspiration the artists shared; but their eyes were focussed on process, and 'the right to fail'—meaning the right to set the terms by which to achieve success—became their cry. It was to be the basis of successive public and private attempts to reconcile the practitioner's need to pursue their process in their own way and the Council's ambition for excellence and commitment to manage the books.

Which brings us to the second intractable problem: the high-minded not-for profit structure. This became a pillar of the new Council, largely because of the dubious record of the AETT in its partnership with the commercial sector Those groups eligible for support had to demonstrate good governance by an honorary board of benevolent citizens who believed in the place of the arts in society. All profits must be recycled into new work. Good taste and a certain educational value was implied and, as things went, a repertoire of too many bankable British or American farces could earn silent reproof in the competition for grants.

This denunciation of the 'commercial' was an entrenched characteristic of Australian theatre which probably derived from the rising middle class's pronounced disdain of the low comedy tradition that had enlivened the countryside from the time of the gold rush; and these feelings had been encouraged in the twentieth century by the aspiring community theatres and the occasional British Council sponsored companies that toured Australia in association with the Australian Elizabeth Theatre Trust. Until quite recently those who worked for JCW, for example, rarely set foot on a government-funded stage. The problems created by this moral guardianship in the early days of subsidy had a much earlier origin.

It was to have unforeseen consequences.

Here I shall pause for a moment to discuss the meaning of the words 'commercial theatre'. In Australia it was, until government supervened, our 'real' theatre entertainment, as opposed to the drama societies sprinkled across the land. The major theatres were proprietory companies that owned property, bought rights to successful shows from the world centres, and reproduced them with a high degree of skill for Australian audiences. Their productions, when successful, showed a great deal of business acumen, technical prowess and marketing skill but very little originality beyond a nose for changing fashion and the taste of their 'good-hearted philistine' audience. The best of them gave us very fine performances, from *My Fair Lady* to *Hair*; and they still do so today.

But their motives had nothing to do with learning, discovery, artist development or gaining understanding of the art of performance. It's about putting on a show. (I refer to the theatre in this paper but what I say applies equally to music and dance.) So the impetus to create our own theatre, interpreting and understanding our own place in the world, came not from the diet of the public theatres but from the amateur theatres inhabited by educated people who understood that the dramatic text, and the act of realising it, had much to offer us in gaining understanding of the ways of the world and our own place in it.

Public theatre, as I choose to call it in the context of this argument, rarely surprises, but can bring to it the mastery that can be achieved only in long-repeated performance. This transforming experience occurs too rarely in our high-art theatre because a long run is so rare and the elements so precious. An insight into how protective some artists continue to feel about art theatre can be found in Robyn Nevin's 2000 Philip Parsons Memorial Lecture in which she inveighs against the Sydney Theatre Company directors' recent practice of partnering with commercial investors. In a footnote she defines what she means by 'commercial':

> *By commercial I mean the programming of plays with the primary intent of achieving a profitable financial outcome. This is not to imply that commercial and artistic outcomes are mutually exclusive but I believe some plays are direct and deliberate commercial choices.*[15]

This is not a definition that can stand up: intent is not evidence; a profitable outcome is surely every producer's hope. Nor does the definition take account of the many elements beside the text that contribute to a profitable outcome. But it does define the powerful emotions that the new subsidised arts had engendered in their practitioners, and which in some circles can still be felt today.

At her time of writing Nevin, today one of our great actors, was the recently appointed director of the Sydney Theatre Company and her paper gives a revealing account of the kind of company she wished to build, of her frustration at the complexities she faced in the process and her disapproval of some of the work of her predecessors, Richard Wherrett and Wayne Harrison, who had joined with public theatre partners for certain productions and earned a profitable outcome in a time of need. As a graduate from the first intake of NIDA in 1960-61, Nevin was the product of two major forces in the 1970s: the Old Tote Theatre, which provided solid work on the classics in a university context and the security of a twelve-month contract; and the Performance Syndicate, Rex Cramphorn's itinerant Grotowski-style experimental workshop which undertook a deep investigation of the text and gave performances only when the work was ready. As a director she also had the support of two State premiers who shared a fellow feeling for the arts.[16] Her imagining of an ideal theatre company, developing and presenting only work of the highest order, reflects these ambitions; but the task proved an onerous one. The short life of her ensemble, the Actors' Company, in the late 2000s, was in the end a testament to the demands we place on our artists, and they on themselves, when, like government, they must confine their work to the art of the possible.[17]

Today the pressures are even greater and the ambitions for 'Australianness,' innovation and profitability as far away as ever. In 2007 Lyndon Terracini, the pioneering founder of the Northern Rivers Performance Arts (NORPA) and at his time of writing director of the Brisbane Festival, put a passionate argument for the importance of place in art, and for the role of community in its creation.[18] In it he called for a breakdown of the barriers between 'high art' and the rough community art in which he saw both cultural continuity and the the crucible of innovation. Since becoming artistic director of Opera Australia in 2010, that company has expanded, opted for commercial partnerships and become a victim of its eminence.

New forms of performance

The approved companies in 1968 saw the plans for a federal funding body as an opportunity to do the work they had always wanted to do: to have a company of actors and the directors, designers, technicians and management structures to support them. We were ready for the challenge in a way we had not been, back in 1954. NIDA was up and running, arts centres were being designed and built, performers were lured home from the UK and the US with 12-month contracts. It was a heady time.

But, of course, the culture was still derivative. Where were the playwrights? What we remember today are not the dedicated productions of the classics (some of which, as I remember it, were 'excellent') but the raffish satirical writers' theatres that sprang up in opposition to the new establishment, a movement that lasted a decade, as such movements do, and whose writers were quickly poached by the mainstages. In shabby premises and with little support these young people, who have come to be called the New Wave, drew their style and inspiration not from the realist theatre then prevailing but from the spirit of protest that pervaded the time, the traditions of home-grown vaudeville and melodrama, and from the many international models of experimental theatre that came by post.

The New Wave did not destroy the old culture, but used those skills and history learned in British repertory theatre to look critically at itself, take a risk, and make a new investment in an Australian way. They threw out the proscenium and instead took over old warehouses, a trades hall, a stable, and created a new shape of theatre, one that invented its own forms, drew on old comedy, music and poetry, and turned their audiences into participants.[19] Out of this fertility came writers prepared first to satirise, then more directly to criticise, the times. Of them all it was David Williamson who made the leap from the fringe to the mainstage early in the 70s and by the end of the decade had demonstrated his pre-eminence as our comedic storyteller, accurately and satirically documenting his audience to themselves. This had never been achieved before to that degree, nor has it since (though Joanna-Murray-Smith is close as interpreter of the present middle-class generation). As the recession of the 1970s put an end to our early thrill of expansion, the phenomenon came to be known in the business as 'the Williamson economy'. Williamson was in fact our first 'commercial' success from the New Wave; but he escaped censure and held his place, unchallenged within the state system until he officially retired, as the guarantor of a profitable outcome.[20]

The emergence of larrikin filmmakers and playwrights from the 1970s, like George Miller and Jack Hibberd, and popular television characters like Paul Hogan, Norman Gunston and later political satirists like Max Gillies and the Doug Anthony Allstars,[21] made it a famous period for full-frontal confrontations with ourselves, on stage, in life and in the media.[22] All this soon began to be tabled, documented and questioned. Academics took up the challenge of self-examination. A fever for the new served to widen the split with the old culture, the old Australia and the new one in the making; and between the old ways of making theatre, still prevailing on the mainstages and the ways of living advanced by the 'alternative' theatre as it came to be known.

One of the sectors to benefit at this time was books and plays about our society. Serious studies were made of our growing film industry—more than have been published in any period since. Currency Press's modest output of plays was set for school study with alarming speed: there was a sense of purpose about some kind of national realisation.

As in the budding film industry, with subsidy came dependence and the duty of guardianship. With money, or its possibility, also crept in a self-imposed caution as those in authority let the allowable level of risk-taking be known. By the 1980s the freedom to fail had become unaffordable. The 1970s had seen the reforms and largesse of the Whitlam period, the hectic inflation brought about by the international oil crisis, followed by a dramatic change of government, heavy calls to austerity and, in the case of the arts, ceiling funding. In 1975, after a long and contentious debate, mainly about the warring claims of 'excellence' (Whitlam's view) versus 'need' (ALP policy) one of the Government's last acts was to establish the Australia Council as a statutory body. Up to this time the behaviour of the Council had been tolerated as an aberration of public service practice. The new Arts Minister, Tony Staley, set reform in motion by commissioning the McKinsey Report into administrative efficiency; overseeing attention to the Public Service Board rule book and downsizing Board and staff positions, starting with the removal of the founding chief executive officer, Jean Battersby.[23] Every move was accompanied by a public chorus of revolt as loud as any that had been heard in the 1960s.

The arts in this period had been well ahead of

government in understanding its aims and finding ways to achieve them. Whitlam as Arts Minister had succeeded in persuading both sides of Parliament that the arts were crucial to the common good and had had bipartisan support from his successor, Tony Staley, in the Fraser Coalition Government. It has not often been so. Leigh Tabrett in her fine Platform Paper (No. 34), *It's Culture, Stupid!* she describes in disheartening detail her dealings with state arts ministers who, in her view, had never been clear about why we subsidise the arts.[24] As head of Arts Queensland, she had seen successive parliamentarians struggle with justification for a government role in the arts and persuade themselves in the end that the arts were of marginal benefit.

By the 1980s the New Wave was facing middle age, the state theatres and orchestras were settled in their shiny arts centres, the subscription system was well entrenched. The Sydney Theatre Company had opened in 1979 under Richard Wherrett, following the bankruptcy of the Old Tote, the first chosen state company, which had expanded too far and fast. The standard of performance and production was assured and adventurous: a new generation of Australian-made directors were taking charge and the preoccupation with the less admirable aspects of Australian life was giving way to writers with a larger palette. Plays were being commissioned: we saw the work of some of our best writers in lavish productions of admirable quality. It was also the great decade of the Australian Opera under Moffatt Oxenbould, with the partnership of Joan Sutherland and Richard Bonynge, Bonynge being appointed musical director in 1976. That was also the year that J.C. Williamson's closed its doors, beaten by changing taste, younger entrepreneurs and the competition of publicly funded entertainment. 1987 also saw the retirement of John Sumner, who had built the Melbourne Theatre Company from its beginnings at Melbourne University in 1959 to its presence at the Arts Centre; and in 1988 the retirement of Alan Edwards, founding director of the Queensland Theatre Company. Together they marked the end of the 'Anglo generation' which had dominated our subsidised theatre to that point. The performing arts had become a sector led by younger personalities, and the change was noted with a new respect.

But management was still caught in their cultural trap. They were unable, or unwilling, to trade into the public theatre; the cost of their rented cultural centres and their 'high production values' had risen. When the first government cuts came, the expanding companies faced a new problem: the need to fund the 'high art' repertoire at the level of excellence aspired to by the directors and demanded by their venues, but a declining ability to exploit them for profit.

Community access

Now, with the departure of the older generation, whose belief in philistine conversion had by then been long defeated, the Australia Council faced a new problem for their mandate: a controversy around their responsibility towards the autonomy of the artist and ownership of the artefact. The Australia Council's goal at the start had been to establish a sustainable infrastructure for the existing performing arts organisations. The traditional structure of professional standards and conditions, copyright and individual ownership went unquestioned, as did the artist's obligation to refresh it with criticism, satire and new form. Now, with the establishment of the Crafts, Aboriginal Arts and Community Arts boards, applications began to arrive from artists to work in communities and for grants to be received and disseminated among a group. This was a direct challenge to the old order and one that extended beyond its definition of art into government's social responsibility for preserving traditional practice, cultural continuity and community good. Tim Rowse describes the problem:

> *Craftspeople working in the community forego the formal support structures available to professional artists in the arts world, they are in a position of having to win credibility and confidence in a situation where the value of art and of the artist is not necessarily accepted, indeed, they are intent on questioning the assumption and putting it to the test, by attempting to reveal the creativity that exists within everyone.*

Here was the real challenge to the management of government patronage and the boundaries, even the aspiration, of excellence. Community art and craft came dangerously near commodification. Rowse goes on:

> *In these words we can trace the emergence of a new form of patronage, in which money does not simply pass from statutory body to the artist or company but must take into account a third party which endorses, or will eventually be asked to endorse, the applicant according to their responsibilities to community interest.*[25]

One aspect of this, to which the Community Arts Board and the Arts in Working Life project were short-lived respondents, was the rise of a regional theatre movement, which originated from the Victorian College of the Arts, whose graduates from 1976 sought out country centres in which to establish a form of theatre company based in the life of a community. Some succeeded for a time, and found a place from which to build. The Murray River Performing Group, in Albury-Wodonga, for example, introduced training in circus skills and in due course mutated into the Flying Fruit Fly Circus. But most had a rocky time gaining community acceptance. Most barely lasted a decade.

The mixture of objectives in these ventures became apparent in the McLeay Report, (1986) by the Federal Government's expenditure committee, keen to implement the ALP policy of community access and answering need. Its first recommendation was clear:

> *Commonwealth arts support policy should aim to democratise culture by ensuring wide and steady community access to a diversity of cultural experiences.*[26]

Part of their plan was to place between the Councillors and the five Boards a Community Cultural Development Unit through which applications would be filtered. By this time, of course, the now-established arts sector was all on the side of high art and saw democracy as a threat to their share of funding.

The 1980s were a volatile period for every aspect of the Council's work as it tried to redefine its responsibilities to the arts while these attempts to recognise community interest remained a sticking point. Guiding the government through this had been Dr Timothy Pascoe, Cambridge and Harvard Business School graduate and former federal secretary of the Liberal Party, as the first executive chair of the Australia Council (1981–84). He abandoned the art form boards and restructured with a focus on being more 'objective'. Application forms became more 'responsible', key performance indicators were introduced, together with the measurement of outcomes such as audience attendance and delivery on schedule. 'Challenge grants' were offered by the Council to match funding from the private sector. Government began to re-define its role in the arts as the management of commodities rather than the maintenance of culture. It encouraged Australians to think in terms of 'investing' in the new and rejecting the past. This was encouraged by the grant system which gave special encouragement to new work.

Meanwhile the cost of the lavish cultural precincts in which they worked—the inspiration of the old-order entrepreneurs—began to build a barrier of 'elitism' between the high-art patrons and the community culture.

The price of being 'excellent' also continued to rise. They began to look about for corporate sponsors. Measurement of value was to become the next big thing.

So began the long tail of rising corporate dependence, and with it the middle management required to seek and service sponsorship. In time the sponsors began to take ownership of their investment: staff tickets, interval receptions, participation in company promotion, public appearances, corporate presentation workshops all became part of the deal. The need to succeed was becoming more urgent, the time to prepare more costly and the freedom to succeed on their own terms a distant dream. This process has been gradual, but today novelty, spectacular design, star actors in revisionist productions of familiar classics, are evidence of loss of energy and a flagging imagination.

As commodity value has overtaken arts management so we have depleted our investment. When we go to the Australian theatre now do we still feel a sense of ownership? What does it change about the way we see ourselves, how we see others, how others see us and how we imagine we appear in their eyes? Do we have any better idea now of 'who we are' than when Donald Horne was writing *The Lucky Country*?

4. A changing population

The aftermath of the social changes in the 1970s and 1980s were particularly visible in the education sector, where the received grammatical wisdom of the European-based curricula began to be affected by a more populist 'play-way' style of learning in secondary schools and universities. One outcome included a reduction in the study of classic literature in favour of fictional work with social relevance. Out of this grew a new industry in popular culture studies, which re-examined in the process what it was to be Australian.

At the same time the stability of our universities was being eroded by loss of tenure in favour of contracts, changes in funding and public policy, culminating from 1984 with the Dawkins Plan which introduced the Higher Education Contribution Scheme (HECS), a deferrable fee for tertiary education, closed Technical and Further Education institutions and forcibly amalgamated universities with Colleges of Advanced Education, or converted the latter into university status. Meanwhile the demographics of our secondary schools were changing as steady immigration from Vietnam, Africa and Asia put pressure on literacy in schools and the mastery of English in universities. Other changes occurred, among them a reduction in music education, once accepted in every school. Today strenuous efforts continue to be made to address this loss in the light of growing evidence of the benefit its practice can bring to the developing brain in disciplines like mathematics and languages.[27]

The years leading to the millennium were full of restless change and foreboding. In 1998 I was looking back despondently at these changes, which had included the introduction of an unhelpful relativism into public debate.[28] One effect of this was to introduce more discursive courses into what had been artisan training in performance and related technical areas like lighting and stage design, costume and property making. These were easier to pack with students and therefore cheaper to teach. Tertiary degrees began to replace certificates and diplomas, theses were added to the curriculum: and in the schools the practice of music, drama and dance tuition was beginning to diminish in favour of lectures, on the ground of cost. In this century Government has moved rapidly to place major performing and other arts academies under university administration.[29] In 1989 I dumped my disgruntlement on Wollongong University:

> *The philosophical upheaval within the universities meant that they were by this time no longer purveying the eternal truths in which my generation believed; government had to seek a practical model elsewhere. They chose the wrong model, the economic model [...] funding diminished, language moved from 'receiving an education' to 'purchasing a degree' [...] Now a new threat to the quality of education is causing further division: the level of literacy and diversity of culture among secondary students today.*[30]

My concern had been for our increasing romance with fiscal efficiencyand the economy (remember Paul Keating's 'J-curve' and 'lovely set of numbers'?) and declining interest in feeding the imagination; but my problems, looking back, were equally due to the extraordinary social changes that were taking place in our society and the world; and to the Government's efforts to accommodate the increased diversity of its citizenship. Nevertheless, the problems of the Australian Curriculum we see in 2015 are the outcome of this diminishing interest in the humanities—the unmeasurable subjects like history, philosophy and the arts—and the practical uses of the creative thinker. Instrumentalist learning is now entrenched.[31] The effect on our culture has been profound.

For a while the doors of the arts centres were open to our writers' satire and social criticism; but as the 1990s progressed debts were mounting and energy was flagging. Epic works by Stephen Sewell asserting the immorality of banking and power politics began to be seen as unnecessarily challenging and their performance questioned. By 1996 Richard Wherrett was complaining we were all seeing too many Australian plays and needed to open our minds to the world and do 'some serious R&R'. By which he meant not rest and recuperation, or even recreation, but 'Research and Risk-taking. Ahead of 'comfortable' theatre.[32] Two years later Neil Armfield, then director of Belvoir, observed a dumbing-down of the imagination and accused the arts of being 'elite'. He also drew attention to the new Prime Minister, John Howard's view, that 'there were no votes in the arts.[33]

Things deteriorated further in the new millennium.

Currency House responded in 2004 with the Platform Papers to give voice to the unease. The first edition was Martin Harrison's *'Our ABC'—a Dying Culture?* following one of the regular reviews of its programming.[34] In 2005 Robyn Archer published her savage observations of a political 'dumbing down' of the nation.[35] The pragmatic years under John Howard brought strong expansion and consolidation of the major arts organisations but little financial recognition of the wave of diverse and energetic independent arts enterprises. In 2007 the ALP won office and set about reform, including establishing a national system of public education. In 2010 Prime Minister Julia Gillard, though confronted by a hung parliament, succeeded in gaining the support of the states for a comprehensive reform of schools' resources and a national curriculum. This was the Gonski Report, headed by the financier David Gonski. It was the major achievement of this quarrelsome period. The ALP lost office in 2013 and since then a further review of these reforms has halted their implementation. At the time of writing much energy is going into justifying the functional 'back to basics' purpose of primary and secondary education.

Regarded as ominously ideological is Recommendation 18:

> *With the exception of literacy, numeracy and ICT*[36] *that continue as they currently are dealt with in the Australian Curriculum, the remaining four general capabilities are no longer treated in a cross-curricular fashion. Critical and creative thinking, personal and social capability, ethical understanding and*

> *intercultural understanding should be embedded only in those subjects and areas of learning where relevant and where they can be dealt with in a comprehensive and detailed fashion.*

This language is deceptive. It suggests only literacy, numeracy and ICT are 'so important' that they need to be studied intensively; and that critical and creative thinking, are optional extras in an overcrowded curriculum, not the tools that direct the proper use of literacy, numeracy and ICT in a civilised society. It does not augur well for any future hopes of raising a creative nation. Or even a relevant one, come to that. An education system that discourages healthy inquiry, imagination and philosophic thought, that encourages aimless mental agility, is a serious matter of public health. It reverts to the thinking of those self-appointed entrepreneurs who in 1968 thought our good-hearted philistine could be bettered by an occasional dose of good European culture.

5. So what about our audiences?

> *When you sit with a child and tell a bedtime story, that is theatre. As you hold up a book and point to the characters in the picture and the child's eyes watch and connect and imaginatively see them at work, playing their roles in the story, that is theatre. Through story we discover the world, we test our experiences, we look inside ourselves by projection into imagined characters imagined worlds [...O]ur theatre is our oldest and purest place of social connection and an absolute index of our civilisation.*[37]

The performing arts, and most particularly theatre and music, especially popular music, are our most immediate expressions of what it is like to be an Australian at this time in our history, and so all these changes: immigration, education and language, war, recession, crime, climate change, are part of the ecosystem from which the artist can draw. Even a bedtime story is a reflection of this and derives not from learned knowledge but from the imagination bred from an absorbed culture. Every day new works are written or composed which reflect this changing climate. I have therefore tried to draw attention to these issues, to how they have affected both the artist's struggle to interpret their own society and the Government's wavering will to fund an arts sector that displays us as a talented, civilised and aware society.

Jørn Utzon, banished from his beloved Opera House in 1966, confided his hopes for the finished work to me at his house in Denmark in 1969. This is how he saw them:

> *[H]e was building his Opera House not for the NSW Government, nor for Australian culture, nor for his own indulgence and certainly not as a monument to anyone; but for the ordinary people of Sydney, to express their life, the freedom and enterprise he found in them, their climate and the constantly changing, surprising and sometimes dangerous qualities of their harbour. [...] The whole complex, as he described it, had a coherent philosophy which began with the life of the city and harbour and drew it towards the stage. There was no light or tile that did not have its place in that philosophy.*[38]

The ordinary people of Sydney have indeed taken ownership of the House, and with gratitude. But how often do those who pack the forecourt and watch the yachts by day and fireworks by night, actually attend the theatres and concert hall? The tickets, like the real estate of Sydney, are now beyond the reach of the average family, nor has the majority of those families much thirsted for the joys offered inside these famous sails or yearned for the pleasure of a national repertoire.

My most prescient recollection of that meeting with Utzon was his imaginative vision of what arriving at the completed Sydney Opera House would be like: the long climb up the Mayan steps into the vaulted concrete foyers and by degrees entering into the auditoria, their colours coalescing as we focus on the stage curtain. Arriving there in my imagination, with all my expectations, my mind could hold only one unspoken question: 'What do we have in Australia to put behind that curtain that could possibly ensure the journey would not end in disappointment?'

In fact we didn't do too badly that first season in 1973. However, John Coburn's Aubusson tapestry curtains of the sun and the moon, woven for the Opera and Drama halls, as they then were, never realised Utzon's vision. They proved too heavy, and latterly too valuable, for practical use. Was that an omen that we were expecting too much?

In the years that followed I came to believe we were unwise to build our temples to the performing arts before we had achieved the skills and strategies that required them. The dazzle of the Sydney Opera House project has distorted our thinking about the process. So we have continued to be importers of others' goods instead of exporters of our own. But it's not too late. In fact the moment is right for change. Its time to place the creative team at the centre of our thinking: recognise them by the work they do; help them build employment opportunity, collaboration and cross-fertilisation. Encourage flexibility, exchange ideas and share experience, instead of placing barriers of regulation and envy in the way of a career path. In short, make our performing arts culture one of process, not product.

A career path is at present a thing unknown to most

practitioners. They do what they do, and there is no succession strategy, no expansion or alternative conceivable beyond the known. Those who built our industry in the subsidised sector have for the most part walked away with their superannuation and no ready work waiting. No stake in the successful productions they delivered—productions that might, in other circumstances, have joined the public circuit and become classics. These are highly qualified personnel but we make no place for them here. The best have done their own career planning, have retrained into other areas, started their own business or been lost abroad.

Being an arts practitioner at all is a risky, uncomfortable business. But it offers special qualities that are intrinsic to a forward-looking creative society. Taking a risk is not foolhardy: it requires judgement, a clear understanding of Australia's 'past and future investment', not just in finite resources like coal and oil but in the infinite resources of the thinking mind. We have brilliant minds, ingenious inventions and extraordinary discoveries that could make this country and this world a better place; but instead we fail for lack of initiative and persistence; quarrel and twitter and vent our frustration on each other. Recognising brilliance in the making requires an instinct for the unexpected. It is a rare and special skill.

If we are ever to produce great playwrights, composers, choreographers, theatre, musicals and films to any noticeable degree, we must learn to trust those who work in art development and give them some latitude. Innovation and risk-taking in any kind of work requires patience: we may not succeed the first time or the second. Most of us can't properly calculate the money or time it takes to build a house, let alone explore an idea.

6. And where are the artists in all this?

In 1970 the British actor Donald Sinden, leading a team to Australia from the Royal Shakespeare Company, expressed surprise at the public's attitude to actors: 'Where is Australia in the soul today?' he asked. 'Actors are honoured in the UK.'[39] We must ask the same question now.

Who are the leaders who speak for their profession? Who are the leaders prepared to be the risk-takers and advocates, to defend 'the right to fail'—and to keep trying for success on their own terms? Society lives on trust: commerce cannot live without it. If you order a cabinet from a furniture maker, you trust it will be delivered in order and on time. If you hail a taxi you expect the driver will take you where you want to go. Equally, your provider trusts you will pay on delivery and in full. If the agreement is broken both sides suffer. So why have the arts allowed themselves to become so inappropriately over-regulated?

It's not a recent problem. One of the contributing causes was the original remit of the Australia Council. A foundation policy decision (a Public Service ruling) was not to answer criticism or engage in public debate.[40] This has in time added to the public's mystification about the creative process and set a precedent which has had consequences. The Council has never seen its role as a spokesman for artists or an advocate, except in private to government. It is not a body that walks beside their client, ie the artist, but preserves a friendly but reserved distance. Nor does their paperwork make concession to the varying capacities of the applicant. People find their way around this but inevitably it encourages neither trust nor confidence.

Nor have we ever encouraged our leading actors to see themselves as leaders. JCW until their last years never cast an Australian in a leading role and in the other theatres the aspirations of the ensemble traditionally held sway. Even today there seems to be a residual reluctance in some theatres to celebrate the actors in a forthcoming production. Bell Shakespeare has had a history of this—an odd characteristic in a repertoire of classics. As I write the radio has been announcing that the arts sector was mourning the death of Stuart Wagstaff, an elegant English actor who settled in Australia in 1958 and spent a long successful career as a personality actor in the public theatre and television. Before tobacco advertising was banned he was a household name as the Benson & Hedges man. Few who grew up in the subsidised community would have known of him.

Today these divisions between the arts and its funding bodies are endemic and the arts themselves have been collusive in widening them. Julian Meyrick, one of our few public intellectuals in the field, recently summed up his exasperation in a private email in the aftermath of the publication of his Platform Paper:

> *I was talking through my PP39 experience with a friend the other night, trying to make sense of some of the over-the-top responses it generated.*[41] *Mine is hardly an isolated case. Pick any issue that's cropped up over the last ten years—women in the theatre, social inclusion, funding reform—and you see the same superficial emotionalism. My generation and the one below it have been crap leaders. There doesn't seem to be any vision beyond the self. We've been so focussed on the personalities that any issue broader is met with tantrums and sulky looks [...]*
>
> *Not everyone is like this, of course; but that's been the tone of the profession and it surely has to change. Look what's happening in the world. What do our fussy, art form differences and vanities really matter? Why on earth aren't we out there pushing our work in all directions at once? True leadership is about managing the questions, not telling people the answer.*[42]

Ralph Myers, in his address, 'The Artistic Director: On the Way to Extinction?' at Belvoir last November, concurred. He sees too many people appointed to arts boards with business skills but no arts practice; who in turn see the answer to sustainability in appointing as artistic directors and creative staff 'people whom they instinctively trust and understand—people like them.'[43] Myers believes the 'creeping replacement of artistic leaders with managers and producers' is an undermining of the collegiate culture that sustains the artist; and a grave threat to the leadership of our artistic life.

> *There is a notable absence of examples of artistic directors behaving like artists. We're spending most of our time pretending to be managers and in keeping our heads down [...] Broadly speaking, there is a nationwide cultural queasiness with artistic leadership, of people being passionate, saying difficult things, and making us think about ourselves.*[44]

This was further endorsed by the Belgian theatremaker Frie Leysen in her keynote address at the 2015 Australian Theatre Forum. She sees Australia's malaise having much in common with Europe.

> *We urgently have to reconsider the role of theatres and festivals, as instruments to facilitate and valorise artists again. And we need more flexible structures, production houses that can work tailor-made with artists. [...] We created a culture of 'pleasing' that is now hijacking us. We want to please everybody: the audience, the subsidisers, the sponsors, the press, the colleagues—a big mistake. Art should not please. On the contrary, art has to show where it hurts in our societies, in our world. We urgently need the courage back to pick up this role of disturber again.*[45]

Though they may be mystified by them, most Australians say they like their arts, that they are part of a civilised society. But the makers find it hard to be a participant. Noni Hazlehurst, a seasoned actor with a powerful belief in the transformative power of which the actor is a custodian, gave an address for Currency House in 2011 on the working life of the actor.[46]

> *So does this work have value? Well, in my view, anything that reminds us that we share more similarities than differences with our fellow human beings has value. Anything that comforts, enlightens, and challenges is valuable. Anything that is memorable because it provided us with solace or insight or empathy or temporarily transported us with delight has value. Anything that shows us that being beautiful, loud, rich and rude is not the only way to succeed, is valuable.*

And on the celebrity that accompanies success she writes, 'Most of us loathe it. We do it because it's in our contracts.' And describes the unrelenting surveillance of one actor she had observed:

> *Heath Ledger is a typical example of a wonderful actor who found the publicity torturous. When we filmed Neil Armfield's* Candy,[47] *Heath was relentlessly hounded while he was trying to work—photographers would leap out from behind trees, in the middle of a take on location, snapping him in his junkie character's wardrobe and make-up, and those photos were printed with captions describing him as dishevelled without any reference to the film. Questions were raised about his personal habits. He was followed to and from work every day. Meanwhile he was trying his best to portray yet*

another extraordinary character in the magnificent body of work he left us. He had no peace and was too gentle a soul to escape being stalked and affected by the press every single day of his too-short life. I have suffered only a tiny fraction of what people like Heath endure, but I have experienced some of the humiliation, vilification, embarrassment and belittlement that the gutter press can cause through their scant regard for the truth. It hurts me and worse, it hurts my family.

The day following, a report of this speech in the *Sydney Morning Herald* sparked a letter to the editor which read:

[T]he lament of Noni Hazlehurst is hilarious [...] Actors are puppets. They do not cure anything, fix anything or create anything. They do as they are told, walk and talk, dress up and enter and leave. Most would be lucky to get a job at the post office if 'acting' hadn't rescued them. Simple as that.[48]

The question raised at the time was: 'Why did the *SMH* editor choose to publish this?' Was it because he/she thought it represented their readership's opinion? This is not an isolated case but its like is more common in the social media than the press.[49] Actors are surrounded by myths and the adulation that follows, but when chinks occur in their wall of privacy, the backlash is rapid. It's not an environment that encourages frank opinion or cultural leadership.

Neither does spending one's youth locked away with a

musical instrument eight hours a day, according to Peter Tregear. Interpretation requires understanding as well as practical ability. Tregear recognised this about his teaching at the ANU School of Music when he defended his unpopular introduction of a liberal arts education for his vocational students:

> *A truly 'elite' tertiary music education will help us not only to produce better musicians, but ultimately people who have something worthwhile to say about what the ultimate purpose of that 'better' might be. Or, to put it more succinctly, such music education will be both accountable to society and consequential for society.*[50]

History is full of examples of great artists who lived difficult, unforgiving, even criminal lives. Obsessive single-mindedness can become psychotic. But Tregear's point is a more contemporary one. He recognises that today only a few of those who graduate from our music and other creative arts schools will go on to have a stellar career on the concert platform or the big screen. Most will become part of the huge business of making, selling and enjoying our arts and entertainment and play their part in the health of our daily lives. It is they on whom we must rely to 'have something worthwhile to say' about our society; we must give them the respect they deserve.

Australia needs its cultural leaders, its generous, understanding and outspoken citizens, as much as we need our obsessive artists.

But I am writing about the perception and practice of the artistic sensibility and the paradoxical place the artist holds in Australian life. One critic thinks we lack imagination at the top. Nick Bryant, a BBC correspondent who recently published an affectionately critical book based on his time in Australia, has called our country a nation of creators that don't think big enough, imagine big enough.

> *Australia's ongoing success can be explained by an updated version of Horne's* Lucky Country *argument. [...W]hat seems like a paradox is actually two sides of the same coin. The very reforms that made the Australian economy so strong contributed to Australian politics becoming so weak. Success has bred complacency, intellectual laziness and pettiness. Canberra was bankrupt, but its impoverishment was a consequence of a politics of prosperity.*[51]

If Bryant is right, and I believe he is, then we have a job ahead of us to better understand our history, to counteract intellectual laziness and update our language. Those trained in the arts and humanities have the qualifications for this but not always the will. The discredited view that Rowse describes of Australian society being 'characterised by a good natured and resourceful philistinism' still prevails in some circles of authority.

I believe we have reached the end of one road and are deeply in need of a change of direction. The moment has come, the talent is straining at the reins. It only awaits government to give a kick to the stirrups. The state theatre companies, Opera Australia, the major orchestras all struggle under the weight of maintenance, expansion and the need to fulfil their obligations. Despite their discounts and their education programs, their ticket prices are within the reach only of the affluent. How does this fulfil the vision of interpreting Australians to themselves through art?

7. So what is the matter with profit?

The germ of what I am about to propose had its conception some years ago when I went with the playwright Alan Seymour, to see the splendid new Parade Theatre at NIDA. Alan was first impressed and then astonished. 'You mean this was built for the students?' And so it was, with a further plan for the profession to mentor the students by performing there themselves. 'Why isn't it a metropolitan theatre?', he asked, 'and the students apprentices?' NIDA was, in fact, founded on the model of a repertory company, and could have continued that way had it not been for the Dawkins merge of institutions like NIDA into the academic modelwork that continues today.[52] The Parade Theatre, seating 700, has been under-used since it opened and is too impractical and expensive for hiring use. The students have two small venues which fit their purpose.

This is just one more example of the edifice complex in action, which since that time has spread to most of our regional cities.[53] If a city arts complex was built as an investment why not make it one? The original investment in buildings like the Arts Centre, Melbourne, and the Opera House, Sydney must have been returned many times by the rents and income from the businesses that have grown up around them. They have also made their social impact: hosted festivals, weddings, school eisteddfods, royal visits, become international tourist icons.

But before I begin, one more clarification. When I refer to better business practice I do not propose surrendering to a commodity culture. My aim has been to question the sector's inherited reluctance to recognise profit as an honest motive and find new ways to give each performance the maximum advantage and life by enabling realistic upfront time and costs, collaboration, investment, shared resources and planning; and good transparent accounting.

Ian Youngs, a BBC arts reporter, in a recent survey of UK theatre, was surprised to find that despite their severe funding cuts from 2009, British theatre was thriving. Back in 1985 director Trevor Nunn had brought down scandal on the Royal Shakespeare Company by partnering with impresario Cameron Macintosh to create *Les Misérables*, the musical. Today the National and other UK subsidised companies are earning millions in royalties from shows they have developed and transferred:

> *There is a premier league of leading subsidised theatre companies that can take their hit shows to the West End, to Broadway and into cinemas, attract private funding and lure top talent. And the gap between that top tier and the other publicly-funded theatres is growing. [...]I was expecting to find a story about theatres cutting production numbers and new writing. What has emerged is a different story [...] they have become more efficient, more resourceful and more entrepreneurial.*[54]

I believe that a genuinely collaborative theatre industry could plan and develop work that would have a longer life than at present is possible. And that there should be a place for every form within it: opera, drama, comedy, dance musicals, circus, children's theatre, puppetry and so on.

Some proposals

What if the not-for-profit status was removed from the equation? What if the Federal Government gave the Major Performing Arts Companies a handshake worth six years' subsidy and told them to rethink their mission, restructure their company and invite investment?[55] State theatres and opera houses could then become metropolitan theatres, available for hire; their maintenance the responsibility of their owner (the State Government). The state companies, now cashed up and relieved of maintenance pressure, could reconsider their work in an atmosphere of new possibility, healthy competition and the profit motive.

Then, what if a national theatre company—or workshop—was available?[56] To select and examine texts, develop productions, run a short try-out season, perhaps a second one, and then put the shows up for auction? The necessary preparation done, they have the opportunity to become part of the major theatres repertoire or be publicly produced, either in the arts centres or the city theatres.

Similarly, why should the subsidised sector not apply their experience also to building a music theatre industry and benefit as an investor? Music theatre generated 1.2 billion in Australia in 2013–14: investment is needed to take the leap forward. John Senczuk in his recent Platform

Paper outlines the long and complex process needed to make a successful musical and proposes Perth as a city with the will and resources to accomplish this.[57]

What would this mean for our 'high art'? Would it mean a rush of popular overseas successes at the expense of local art? It's a possibility for a while but with the revival of a risk-taking culture, new opportunities for collaboration, employment, and the development of work to greater fulfilment, together with new places in which to play, would not the whole landscape of work practice be transformed?

The key to this is the artistic director. The sign of a healthy theatre is an artistic director with an identifiable purpose, who is seen, heard and answerable to the company and the public, and is unquestionably the cornerstone of a collegiate organisation.[58] Otherwise to all the members it becomes a job. Today the annual seasons too often look like the work of a committee allocating the budget: a classic or two, a star or two, a hit comedy or drama and a cautious exploration of some new or near-new local works.

What then would the Australia Council be doing in this scenario? Investing in innovation and quality at all levels: supporting the national theatre workshop, sustaining our tradition and community, and developing high-risk individual talent. Addressing artists' needs by supporting them with travel and work projects, subsidising research, risk-taking and long-term development; answering needs other than major production.

Here are my proposals:

1. A real industry. *I believe that we have the potential for a profit-based performance industry of the highest quality.*

At present we have large state theatre companies and national opera and ballet. And medium-level companies with their own theatres of varying capacity; and a repertoire individual to themselves. Our small public industry is largely excluded from the art .centres, their newer theatres are mostly limited by being attached to casino complexes; and the remaining JCW theatres are shabby. If a level of interchange and collaboration could be achieved in terms of long-term national investment, the resources would go much further.

2. National development. *I believe that we need a national theatre workshop dedicated to developing an Australian performance tradition and working with playwrights to bring the text, performance and design to its optimum before public performance.*

Such a workshop, with its own residential facilities and theatre space away from the major city centres, could reduce the cost and intensity of rehearsal timetables and produce a finished blueprint for a designated company or the market. The present developmental programs are single purpose initiatives and have limited capacity to engage in long-run development. In the proposed environment it could in time grow its own studio audience.

3. Rethought venues. *I believe that it is now time for our performing arts centres to become metropolitan theatres open for hire.*

While they would still have their home in their

arts centre, the state companies could also be free to choose other locations, and try out some of their work in smaller centres before expanding to their regular season. I believe the arts centres should become 'second step' houses, capable of expanding a work from a small theatre to a large one; one that has the resources to display the goods of which our playwrights, directors, choreographers and performers are capable. The brief should include participating in the work of the national workshop enterprise established to develop and tour the Australian repertoire.

4. Refocussed Australia Council. *I believe that the Australia Council should be redrafted to invest their money in talent, employment, assisting individual artists, funding innovation and advancing the interests of cultural continuity and self-examination. Supporting the national workshop would be one of its responsibilities.*

In setting up the Australia Council there was little risk, or expectation outside normal industry practice; the vision was authentic but neither practical at the time nor nationally challenging. To date the Council's history has been one of experiment and change in their management of the professional arts but of very little daring in the development of creative process.

5. Cultural leadership. *I believe that our major artists should take their place at the head of the profession as advocates and spokesmen and women; should actively promote their industry's practice and social value; and be retained by and identified with their particular arts organisation or* *company not through occasional appearances but for a year at a time.*

Cate Blanchett set an example as both co-artistic director and star of the Sydney Theatre Company. An executive position is not required but a Board position should be, from which they could speak as an informed and eloquent representative of an important company and responsible profession.

6. Outside funding. *I believe that the Australian performing arts have more than enough talent and vision to attract their second-step development venture capital and the ethical investment sector.*

Having been forced into a monetarist system by rising costs, our performance companies have learnt to exercise their talents in a commercial environment, have sought out investors, been judged by the quality, reach and price of their product. Their greatest asset, the one that has brought this about, is the innate value they offer both business and the nation—the unique talent of their artists. It is a gift that money cannot buy but can be awarded, and rewarded, if the conditions are right.

My proposals are not prescriptive, just ruminations on what could be possible, and aimed at making the most of all the initiatives already happening in our wide brown land, breaking down the frustrations that derive from uncertainty and the constraints imposed by a long held belief in the separation of art and commerce.

So, how to we begin?

First by facing the past and recognising that working harder on the same treadmill will not change the outcome. Nor can we go on asking Government to 'do something'. The Australia Council has taken some giant steps to re-examine its processes and we shall see what comes of that. But it's time the arts sector itself took charge of its past, present and future.

The Federal Government has never accepted a brief to understand the arts; and few members have had more than a consumer interest. Nor should we have expected more. The Australia Council was engineered by a group of Canberra entrepreneurs faced with a failing public institution responsible for a disparate collection of semi-amateur organisations; who in an unprepared but politically astute stroke achieved the basis for an NGO that could control and direct the spending of government money on the arts.

The immediate consequence was a burst of creativity that has become legendary, which wore itself out naturally, and was followed by other bursts. Meanwhile the states were building an infrastructure for a new high-art industry: arts centres and precincts; and major companies with established infrastructure. There has been only one moment in our political history when the proposition was put to Parliament—and accepted—that the innovation the arts can offer should be at the centre of government thinking. This was Whitlam's Australia Council and the moment ended abruptly and in rage. But the evidence is that had things turned out differently the thinking would still have faded as quickly. There was a less contentious moment in 1993 when Prime Minister Keating released the *Creative Australia* document and his

Creative Fellowships. But they too left little trace.

It's time to face the fact that Government will never be more generous and sponsors less problematic. It is time to put aside the inherited prejudice against 'commercial' theatre and see how it could be made good business practice. The secret lies not in supervising the purchase of materials—or roses—but in the integrity of the creative team in sharing an understanding of the work they do: what is commodity and what is art. It is time for the fifty-year review Wesley Enoch has called for; to examine how we got into this mess; ask ourselves what our core aim really is; take a stand, speak truth to government, assert the right to be independent and go after it.

8. Cultural value and economic good

So, after grappling to understand where the journey of public responsibility for the performing arts has taken us over the past forty-six years, I turned for relief to Jane Gleeson-White's marvellous book, *Double Entry: How the merchants of Venice shaped the modern world—and how their invention could make or break the planet.*[59] Surprisingly, its subject is the history of double entry bookkeeping, but of much more than that; and it has a lesson from history for those who work in the arts: that good business practice and the generous management of profit is as much responsible for the health and quality of a culture as artistic merit. Luca Pacioli, Franciscan monk and celebrated mathematician, author of the first treatise on double entry, was also a friend of the painter Piero della Francesca, who may have taught him mathematics; and of Leonardo da Vinci to whom he may have taught mathematics. Maths, science, art, magic and astrology were all part of the same knowledge base in those days—and the same practice.

Before double entry, a merchant's finance was recorded in a single journal, a simple record of transactions. The revelation came with the division of income and expenses into two columns, and the recording of a purchase as increasing both debt and capital. This produced for the first time the bottom line, that determined profit and loss and revealed the joy of disposable income.

From such rose the palaces of Venice, and the culture of the Renaissance.

> *It turned out that just as the wealth of Renaissance Italy was underpinned by a new method of book-keeping, so the art of some of the greatest painters of the age was underpinned by mathematics—and Luca Pacioli was implicated in both revolutionary arguments.*[60]

Pacioli's method soon spread across Europe and the known world; and was by degrees refined.[61] No other method has ever superseded it.

We in the arts need to know this. And governments need to know that it was the wealth of the nation, not its accounting of it, that created the Renaissance and the benefits of learning, science and philosophy that built what we call a civilised society. It was only in the nineteenth century, with the Industrial Revolution and rise of the corporations, that accountancy was first recognised as a profession, that government regulation began to be felt by private enterprise and conflicts of interest entered the conversation. The slide into the Great War in 1914, followed by the Great Depression in 1929, set the western world thinking that unfettered capitalism might not be best way to conduct a society and that some form of national accounting was needed. Maynard Keynes' *General Theory of Employment, Interest and Money* (1934) provided a theoretical basis for the first national accounts of assets and expenditure—and led inexorably to the introduction of one of the most powerful and misleading tools of modern government, the Gross Domestic Product.

So began the evangelism of measurement. The GDP was useful while the wealth of a nation was simply unknown; and it flourished in the post-Second World War boom of consumerism. But by 1968 Robert Kennedy in his heart-wrenching speech at the University of Kansas three months before his assassination, was inveighing against the moral decline of his country and the malign influence of the GDP. It begins:

> *[F]or too long we seemed to have surrendered personal excellence and community values in the mere accumulation of material things [..]*

And it ends:

> *It [the GDP] does not include the beauty of our poetry or the strength of our marriages, the intelligence of our public debate or the integrity of our public officials. It measures neither our wit nor our courage, neither our wisdom nor our learning, neither our compassion nor our devotion to our country, it measures everything in short, except that which makes life worthwhile. It can tell us everything about America except why we are proud that we are Americans.*[62]

The principles of the GDP, unlike Pacioli's method,

have outlasted their usefulness and have taken our world in the wrong direction. It was a product of consumerism, a contrivance brought about by the wars and deprivation of the first half of the twentieth century, and the post-war glut of home ownership and domestic appliances. It was then accelerated by the decade of open markets and the arrival of the internet, making it still harder to relate this new materialism to moral values and social cohesion, as Kennedy describes them.

Harvard philosopher Michael Sandel sees this as a major problem for our age:

> *Something bigger is at stake. The most fateful change that unfolded during the past three decades was not an increase in greed. It was the expansion of markets and of market values, into spheres of life where they don't belong. To contend with this condition, we need to do more than inveigh against greed, we need to rethink the role that markets should play in our society. We need a public debate about what it means to keep markets in their place. To have this debate, we need to think through the moral limits of markets. We need to ask whether there are some things money should not buy.*[63]

The creative sector and the community know this, just as they know that climate change is real as a social threat as well as a physical one; and should be leading both debates. Sandel's book is a litany of horrors of American life today, where every aspect of good, generous citizenship has been perverted by a bribe or a reward. The fact that he makes it an entertaining read makes it all the more ominous.

The subsidised arts sector in Australia has for forty years made a moral virtue of being not-for-profit, by which they demonstrate their dedication to putting art at the centre of their working life. At the start it was a way of protecting the public money from unexplainable uses; but it came to be expected, then demanded and depended upon. Today the work is no longer knowingly unprofitable. It has just been contracted out. The time is overdue to discard the moral haze that has prevented innovatory business practice from making a creative contribution to the arts in our society.

This turbulent period of transition through which we are living will very soon reach a tipping point. And for that reason it offers a unique opportunity to those who work in the creative sector to pause and rethink their contribution to society, to consider what Peter Tregear has written about the need for performers to be more than practitioners: to take their place as informed citizens in public life. Time to think about being better communicators and advocates; to think beyond the personal; ask questions and give thoughtful, informed answers. Time to stop allowing managers to dictate our creative life. It's time to call for change in our own way and if you believe in what you say don't leave it others, to the Government, to make the running. If you like the ruminations in this paper, then let's hear from you. If you hate the proposals, don't just dismiss them: give us your reasons and let's find a better way. Show Meyrick, Pledger and Tregear there is vision among practitioners beyond the self.

Now is the right time for some serious R&R. Let's have the debate that Michael Sandel is asking for: and prove that our creative thinkers and doers are the custodians of all those things that money should not buy.

Endnotes

1. Robyn Archer, *The Myth of the Mainstream: Politics and the performing arts in Australia today.* Platform Papers 4, April 2005 p.32.
2. Harriet Parsons, 'Growth and Depression in Hayek's Garden: The emotional language of accounting' in *Making Culture Count: The Politics of Cultural Measurement,* edited by Marnie Badham and Lachlan MacDowall (University of Melbourne), with Emma Blomkamp (University of Melbourne/University of Auckland) and Kim Dunphy (Cultural Development Network/Deakin University, Melbourne: Palgrave Macmillan, forthcoming.
3. Donald Horne, *The Lucky Country,* Melbourne: Penguin Books, first published 1964, sixth edition 2008, pp.228–9.
4. The *Australian* began publishing in 1964 and I succeeded Francis Evers as national theatre critic in 1967. I wrote two columns a week and occasional features; and it was a part-time job for this mother of two to cover all the capital cities.
5. Wesley Enoch, *Take Me to Your Leader: The dilemma of cultural leadership',* Platform Papers 40, August 2014 p.56.
6. The previous venue was the Town Hall and season tickets were so scarce the story went that they were named by some subscribers in their will.
7. Eduard Borovansky was a Czech singer and character dancer who with his wife had been caught in Australia at the outset of World War II after touring with the Russian Ballet de Monte Carlo. They set up a ballet school and launched the Borovansky Ballet in 1940 presenting a repertoire of familiar European classics.
8. Vance Palmer, introduction to *Louis Esson and the Australian theatre.* Melbourne, Georgian House 1948. Quoted by John McCallum in Philip Parsons (gen. ed. with Victoria Chance) *Companion to Theatre in Australia,* Sydney, Currency Press 1995.
9. Kath Leahy, *Lords and Larrikins: The Actor's role in the making of Australia.* Sydney: Currency House 2009.
10. Stars Peter Finch, Keith Michell, Zoe Caldwell, Leo McKern, Joan Sutherland, Patricia Conolly, Robert Helpmann, director Michael Blakemore, were some of those who went abroad and made their name at this time.
11. Philanthropy via tax deduction was not encouraged then as it is

today. But the Trust had a useful exemption which was widely utilised. If you sent them a cheque with a note saying: 'I'm interested in the work of a certain music group' the money would in due course reach its destination minus a fee of one or two per cent.

12. Tim Rowse, *Arguing the Arts: The funding of the arts in Australia.* Sydney: Penguin 1965, p.9.
13. Julian Meyrick, 'We might call these the Anglo generation, not because they were all English, but because they consciously borrowed their working methods from the British theatre of the time, particularly the better class of regional repertory company.' *See How it Runs. Nimrod and the New Wave.* Sydney: Currency Press 2002, pp.4–5:
14. The Method, as Lee Strasberg's style of acting came to be known, is an American derivative of the Stanislavsky method. It was very new to Australia when Hayes opened his in-the-round boatshed theatre in 1959. 'The Method trains actors to use their imagination, senses and emotions to conceive of characters with unique and original behaviour, creating performances grounded in the human truth of the moment.' *What is Method acting*? http://newyork.methodactingstrasberg.com/what-is-method-acting/
15. 'Robyn Nevin, Getting to Know the Theatre and Imagining What It Might Be' in *The Parsons Lectures 1993–2003,* Currency House 2003, p.108 fn17.
16. NSW Premiers Neville Wran (1976–86) were responsible for the development of the Wharf Theatre, and Bob Carr (1995–2005) for the Sydney Theatre.
17. See James Waites, *Whatever Happened to the STC Actors Company?* Platform Papers 23, April 2010.
18. Lyndon Terracini, *A Regional State of Mind: Making art outside metropolitan Australia,* Platform Papers 11, January 2007.
19. This improvised open-stage architecture has been embodied by most of the theatres built in Australia since that time and is one of the defining qualities of Australian theatre today.
20. Williamson has nevertheless had a long-running stand-off with the theatre press reviewers. Perhaps they share this curious guilt about popular success.
21. Paul Hogan was a rigger on the Sydney Harbour Bridge who became a popular TV comedian and in 1986 star of the hit movie *Crocodile Dundee.* Norman Gunston was the TV creation of the actor Gary McDonald, an inept but determined TV newsman who subverted visiting celebrities by persuading them of his authority. The Doug Anthony Allstars were a trio of singers and satirists with an aggressive political agenda. Their members are probably better remembered today than the bluff Leader of the National Country

Party after whom the group was named.

22. *Countdown* (1974–86) was one notable example: an ABC TV Sunday night pop music show hosted by Ian (Molly) Meldrum, a man of extraordinary knowledge and skill at picking talent, and which over a decade achieved international status for many Australian stars.
23. See Justin Macdonnell, *Arts, Minister? Government Policy and the Arts.* Sydney: Currency Press 1992.
24. Leigh Tabrett, *It's Culture, Stupid! Reflections of an arts bureaucrat.* Platform Papers 34, February 2013.
25. Rowse, pp.25, 26.
26. See Philip Parsons (ed) *Shooting the Pianist: the Role of Government in the Arts.* Sydney: Currency Press 1987; a collection of papers from a one-day seminar held at the University of NSW on 25 October 1986 to debate the contents of *Patronage. Power and the Muse, Inquiry into Commonwealth assistance to the Arts.* Report from the House of Representatives Standing Committee on Expenditure, September 1986.
27. See Robert Walker, *Beethoven or Britney? The Great Divide in Music Education,* Platform Papers 20, April 2009. On pp.6–11 the author lists a host of international studies showing the beneficial effect upon cognitive studies and social skills, of music as part of the curriculum. Music Council of Australia also publishes research, most recently Chris Bowen, , http://musicaustralia.org.au/2014/10/new-research-shows-that-music-lessons-enhance-brain-function/
28. Relativism, the assertion that everything is relative to some framework of understanding and there is no received definition of good or evil.
29. The Victorian College of the Arts became an affiliate of the University of Melbourne in 1991 and a Faculty in 2007; the Canberra School of Music was more radically taken over by the Australian National University with a retrenchment of staff in 2012. Both were accompanied by mass public protest. See Richard Murphet, *The Fall and Rise of the VCA,* Platform Papers 28, July 2011; and Peter Tregear, *Enlightenment or Entitlement? Rethinking tertiary music education,* Platform Papers 38, February 2014. The WA Academy of the Performing Arts is now part of Edith Cowan University. NIDA is situated on the University of NSW campus but its constitution has so far prevented a takeover.
30. Paper delivered at the University of Wollongong Creative Arts Conference 9–11 September 1998.
31. Instrumentalism: a form of pragmatism which maintains that the function of thought is to be instrumental to control of the environment and that ideas have value according to their function in

human experience or progress. *Macquarie Dictionary.*

32. Richard Wherrett, 'some Serious R&R', in *The Parsons Lectures 1993-2003.* Currency House 2003 p.67.
33. Neil Armfield, 'Australian Culture: creating it and Losing It', in *The Parsons Lectures 1993-2003.* Currency House 2003 pp.88–92.
34. July 2004. It argued that the ABC was not fulfilling its Charter obligations to the arts and informed debate. Instead it was steadily popularising with talk back and pop music.
35. Robyn Archer, *The Myth of the Mainstream: Politics and the performing arts in Australia today.* Platform Papers 4, April 2005.
36. Information and Communication Technologies—ie computer literacy.
37. Neil Armfield, 'Australian Culture: Creating and Losing It' in *The Parsons Lectures 1995–2003,* Sydney: Currency House 2003, pp.84–5
38. Katharine Brisbane, *Australian,* 27 December 1969, reproduced in *Not Wrong—Just Different: Observations on the rise of contemporary Australian theatre.* Sydney: Currency Press 2005. p.113.
39. Katharine Brisbane, Interview with Donald Sinden, *Australian,* 4 April 1970.
40. They do issue reviews and policy reports, even discussion papers; but do not participate in public commentary.
41. Julian Meyrick, *The Retreat of our National Drama*, Platform Papers 39, May 2014.
42. Meyrick, email to the author, 15 August 2014. Published with the author's permission.
43. Ralph Myers, Philip Parsons Memorial Lecture, 'The Artistic Director; on the Way to Extinction?' Belvoir Street Theatre, Sydney, 30 November 2014, http://belvoir.com.au/news/artistic-director-way-extinction/
44. See also David Pledger, *Re-valuing the Artist in the New World Order,* Platform Papers 36, August 2013.
45. Frie Leysen, 'Embracing the Elusive', *ArtsHub* 5 February 2015 at http://www.artshub.com.au/news-article/opinions-and-analysis/all-arts/embracing-the-elusive-247065
46. Noni Hazlehurst, *You Know Everything about Me and Nothing about Me.* Speech in the Currency House Arts and Public Life Breakfast Series, 26 October 2011 at https://currencyhouse.org.au/search/node/Noni%20Hazlehurst%20speech.
47. *Candy* (2006), a drama about heroine addiction, directed by Neil Armfield, with Heath Ledger and Abbie Cornish and in which Noni Hazlehurst, played a role. Ledger (1976–2008) died in New York from an overdose of prescription medication, believed to have been related to the effects on his mind and body of his role as the

psychopathic Joker in the Batman movie *The Dark Knight* released that year.

48. *Sydney Morning Herald* 28 October 2011.
49. Sarrah Le Marquand, 'Leave Carbon Cate Blanchett alone', *Telegraph* (Sydney) 30 May 2011, gives some account of the attention Blanchett received for appearing in a TV commercial asking the public to support the proposed carbon price. http://blogs.news.com.au/dailytelegraph/sarrahlemarquand/index.php/dailytelegraph/comments/leave_carbon_cate_blanchett_alone/
50. Peter Tregear, *Enlightenment of Entitlement: Rethinking tertiary music education:* Platform Papers 38, February 2014, p.55.
51. *The Rise and Fall of Australia: How a great nation lost its way.* North Sydney: Random House Bantam Books 2014, p.147.
52. The Victorian College of the Arts became an affiliate of the University of Melbourne in 1991 and a Faculty in 2007; the Canberra School of Music was more radically taken over by the Australian National University with a retrenchment of staff in 2012. Both were accompanied by mass public protest. See Richard Murphet *The Fall and Rise of the VCA,* Platform Papers 28, July 2011; and Peter Tregear, *Enlightenment or Entitlement? Rethinking tertiary music education,* PP38, February 2014. The WA Academy of Performing Arts (WAAPA) is now part of Edith Cowan University. NIDA is on the campus of the University of NSW but was saved from acquisition by its constitution.
53. A good proportion of these centres were the subject of local controversy at the time of building—the Port Macquarie Glasshouse is a celebrated example—and continue to have difficulty with continuous programming.
54. Ian Youngs, *BBC News Arts and Entertainment* 15 February 2015, at http://www.bbc.com/news/entertainment-arts-30880012
55. The six-year funding was a proposal made by Leigh Tabrett in Platform Papers 34, *It's Culture, Stupid! Reflections of an arts bureaucrat,* p.51. In 2015 the Australia Council has announced a six-year funding program. However, the purpose is still aimed at artistic output and the funding will be disbursed progressively.
56. See a proposal by Julian Meyrick in Platform Papers 39, *The Retreat of Our National Drama,* pp.73-6.
57. John Senczuk, *The Time is Ripe for the Great Australian Musical,* Platform Papers 42, February 2015.
58. Wesley Enoch in *Take Me to Your Leader,* tells of a four-year review of the Royal Shakespeare Company to address the 'entrenched hierarchy' and make work and pay conditions more equitable. The outcome, according to the Demos report, was transforming. Platform Papers 40, August 2014 pp.57–9.

59 Jane Gleeson-White, *Double Entry*. Sydney: Allen & Unwin, second edition 2012.
60. Jane Gleeson-White, *Double Entry,* Sydney: Allen & Unwin, second edition 2012, p.7.
61. Luca Pacioli, *Particularis de computis et scripuris* (Particulars of Reckonings and Writings) was published as part of his mathematical encyclopaedia in Venice in 1494.
62. Robert F Kennedy, speech to the University of Kansas, 18 March 1968, http://conversableeconomist.blogspot.com.au/2012/01/robert-kennedy-on-shortcomings-of-gdp.html
63. Michael J. Sandel, *What Money Can't Buy: The moral limits of markets* New York: Farrer, Strauss and Giroux, 2012, p.7.

FORTHCOMING

PP 44, August 2015
CULTURAL PRECINCTS: ART OR COMMODITY?
Justin Macdonnell

Worldwide an estimated $250 billion will be spent in the current decade on creating 'cultural precincts'. The trend started in the US in the 1980s and has spread like wildfire. In essence these are clusters of buildings and spaces with some arts-related function: museums, galleries, concert halls, theatres. What is their purpose? There's evidence that they sell more tickets but none that their art is better. Property values rise but are artists better rewarded? Does the public have a richer experience or just a more convenient one? Could their impact even be counter-productive?

AT YOUR LOCAL BOOKSHOP FROM 1 AUGUST
AND AS A PAPERBACK OR ON LINE
FROM OUR WEBSITE AT
WWW.CURRENCYHOUSE.ORG.AU

Copyright Information

PLATFORM PAPERS
Quarterly essays from Currency House Inc.
Founding Editor: Dr John Golder
Currency House Inc. is a non-profit association and resource centre advocating the role of the performing arts in public life by research, debate and publication.

Postal address: PO Box 2270, Strawberry Hills, NSW 2012, Australia
Email: info@currencyhouse.org.au Tel: (02) 9319 4953
Website: www.currencyhouse.org.au Fax: (02) 9319 3649

ISBN 978 0 9924890 4-5
ISSN 1449-583X

Typeset in Garamond
Printed by Lightning Source
Production by XOU Creative

Printed in Australia
AUOC02n1219270315
266646AU00009B/11/P

9 780992 489045